FLOWERS AND FURNITURE IN AMERICA'S HISTORIC HOMES

FLOWERS AND FURNITURE IN AMERICA'S HISTORIC HOMES

annotated by Elfreda Finch

foreword by
Angela Place, Vice-Chairman
of the National Trust
for Historic Preservation

HEARTHSIDE PRESS, INC., Publishers • New York

THE HOUSES

FOREWORD

It may seem strange in this foreword for *Flowers and Furniture in America's Historic Homes* to read about the National Trust for Historic Preservation in the United States. There is, however, a very real dialogue between the National Trust and flowers.

The National Trust for Historic Preservation was founded in 1949 to preserve the historic houses of America and keep them for posterity as a living page of history. It is the only national service organization privately supported for the public good, the only national private group chartered by the Congress of the United States that is directed to help preserve sites, buildings, and objects significant in American history and culture. We have destroyed so much of our country that an organization such as the National Trust was really essential to further preservation. Almost as soon as the Trust was founded, it became the possessor of several houses, all of great distinction. The first house, I believe, was Woodlawn, built by George Washington for his nephew, Lawrence Lewis, and his bride. This house, through the generosity of the Garden Club of Virginia, now has a very beautiful garden of the period. However, one of its greatest charms is beautiful flower arrangements throughout the house. It has always seemed to me that flowers in a historic house which is not lived in brings the house to life and takes you back in history to the days it was filled with an active family.

To all of us who are interested in historic preservation, it will be of the greatest help to have available this charming book listing historic houses all over the United States. In a few succinct paragraphs this book gives the history of each house. Also, to have such a book available will make many people who delight in creating flower arrangements know what houses are being preserved in their neighborhood and from reading this book I am convinced that many offers to put flowers in these fine houses will come to the custodians of each house.

The membership of the National Trust is increasing rapidly and with this increase comes a larger and larger attendance at historic houses owned and administered by the National Trust. I am sure as the interest in visiting historic houses grows the houses that have beautiful flowers throughout them will make the greatest appeal.

ANGELA MOORE PLACE
(Mrs. Hermann G. Place)

PHOTOGRAPHIC CREDITS

This book could not have been published without the active and generous assistance of a great many people. We are deeply grateful to the members of the garden clubs, the curators and administrative staffs of the historic houses, the press-bureau staff, and the photographers. Among those whose names were known to us are:

Bartow-Pell Mansion—Mrs. Morgan A. Casey; photography by L. H. Frohman.   Bellingrath Gardens and Home—Mr. Fred W. Holder.   William Blount Mansion—Mrs. J. S. Dempster; photography by Snelson Art Studio; flower arrangements by Knoxville Garden Club of the Garden Club of America. Brush-Everard House—Miss Marguerite Gignilliat; photography by Colonial Williamsburg.   Boscobel—Mr. Frederick W. Stanyer.   John Brown House—Mr. Clifford P. Monahon.   Casa Amesti—National Trust for Historic Preservation; photography by Burgess.   Thomas Cooke House—photography by Mrs. Tudor Finch.   Corbit-Sharp House—Horace L. Hotchkiss, Henry Francis du Pont Winterthur Museum.   Lowell Damon House—Mrs. Ervin G. Krueger.   Decatur House—National Trust for Historic Preservation.   The Elms—Mrs. Leonard J. Panaggio, The Preservation Society of Newport County.   Frick Mansion—Mr. Edgar Munhall.   Governor's Palace—Miss Marguerite Gignilliat; photography by Colonial Williamsburg; B. Altman & Co. for pressed flower pictures. Hopkins House—Mrs. Robert Spencer Preston; photography by Laurence E. Tilley.   Stan Hywet Foundation—Kate Clapp of the Akron *Beacon Journal;* photography by Ted Walls.   Longfellow's Wayside Inn—Mr. Francis Koppes; photography by John F. McGovern.   Low House—Mrs. John Wright Carswell; photography by Williams Studio.   Lyndhurst—Mrs. Alda Watson; photography by L. H. Frohman.   Macculloch Hall—photography by Molly Adams.   Metropolitan Museum of Art—Gift of the members of the committee of the Bertha King Benkard Memorial Fund, 1946; gift of Mrs. J. Insley Blair, 1948.   Morven—Isabel Brooks; photography by Mrs. John C. Bayles. Museum of Fine Arts, Boston—photography by Frederick G. S. Clow.   National Trust for Historic Preservation—Mr. J. William Bethea.   Oatlands—National Trust for Historic Preservation.   Olana —Mr. William G. Tyrrell, New York State Historic Trust; photography by Wayne Andrews.   Old Sturbridge Village—Mr. James J. Keeney; photography by Old Sturbridge Village News Bureau. Philadelphia Museum of Fine Arts—Mr. Hobart Lyle Williams, Philadelphia Museum of Art; flower arrangements by the Garden Club of America.   Edgar Allan Poe Museum—Mrs. Edward Hamilton Bryson, Virginia Chamber of Commerce; photography by Jim Corbett; flower arrangements by Thomas Jefferson Garden Club.   Rosedown—Miss Ola Mae Word; Mr. Bradley Little and *Architectural Digest;* photography by Max Eckert.   Nathaniel Russell House—Mrs. S. Henry Edmunds; photography by Kathleen A. Riley.   Schuyler-Hamilton House—photography by David W. Bodle and Pauline S. Bodle.   Seward House—Mrs. Bruce E. Lewis; photography by Andrew Tarby.   Tyron Palace—Mrs. Gertrude S. Carraway; photography by Wray Studio.   Van Cortlandt Manor—Mrs. Catherine Thornton, Sleepy Hollow Restorations; photography by McFall.   Viscaya—Mr. Jefferson T. Warren; photography by Miami-Metro News Bureau.   Waterloo Village—photography by Mrs. Tudor Finch and Horn/Griner.   Westbury Gardens and Home—Mrs. Etienne Boegner.   White House—Miss Elizabeth Carpenter; photography by Robert L. Knudsen and Abbie Rowe.   Tempe Wick House—National Park Service.   Wilcox House—Mrs. John G. Simonds, Mrs. George P. Wagoner; flower arrangements by members of Old York Garden Club.   Winterthur Museum—Dorothy W. Greer, Mr. Ian M. G. Quimby; Henry Francis du Pont Winterthur Museum.   Woodlawn Plantation—National Trust for Historic Preservation; photography by Baptie.   George Wythe House—Miss Marguerite Gignilliat; photography by Colonial Williamsburg.

FLOWERS AND FURNITURE IN AMERICA'S HISTORIC HOMES

MACCULLOCH HALL
MORRISTOWN, NEW JERSEY — CLASSIC REVIVAL

George Perot Macculloch was an accomplished Scotch linguist who came to America in 1808 when his mercantile business was affected by the Napoleonic Wars. Here in 1806 he opened a fashionable Latin School for Young Gentlemen, Macculloch Hall. The Hall, which was acquired in 1949 by the Hon. W. Parson Todd, is today owned and operated by the Todd Foundation, which provides for its care and maintenance and makes it available to various organizations for meetings.

Below   The attractive entrance hall features a portrait of Washington by Charles Willson Peale. On the piano is an arrangement by Mrs. Harold Pletcher of carnations, ranunculus, tuberoses, and snapdragons in tones of pink and gold to harmonize with the gold wallpaper. On the dolphin-legged table, Mrs. Donald Smith uses *Eleagnus pungens* "Simoni," golden *Chamaecypris obtusa* "Crippsi," and bronze to gold chrysanthemums in a soft gray vase. The harp, 75 years old, belonged to the Todd family.

LONGFELLOW'S WAYSIDE INN
SOUTH SUDBURY, MASSACHUSETTS — c. 1700

The Inn began as a two-room affair, one above the other. It was built about 1700 by a grandson of John Howe, first of the line in America who had pushed westward from Waterton and settled in Sudbury. He had the consent of the selectmen of Sudbury "to keep a house of entertainment for travelers if the honored justices think meet," according to a petition to His Majesty's Justices of the Court of the Sessions at Concord.

During the next sixteen years the population of the beautiful Connecticut Valley increased, roads were improved, and stagecoaches began to run, so David Howe added two more rooms. By 1740, its successive owner Colonel Ezekiel Howe had added four more rooms to the rear of the establishment, covering the whole structure with a gambrel roof. As leader of the local minutemen, the colonel led two companies of the Sudbury militia to the Battle of Concord, and one of his sons, Ezekiel, Jr., fought bravely at the Battle of Saratoga where he was severely wounded.

Famous in Revolutionary War days, the inn became even more famous in the 1850's when Longfellow used it as the setting for *Tales of the Wayside Inn*. Much as the poet saw it then, so we see it today:

The firelight shedding over all
The splendor of its ruddy glow
Filled the whole parlor large and low
It gleamed on waistcoat and on wall,
It touched with more than wonted grace
Fair Princess Mary's pictured face;
It bronzed the rafters overhead,
On the old spinet's ivory keys
It played inaudible melodies,

It crowned the somber clock with flame,
The hands, the hours, the maker's name,
And painted with a livelier red
The landlord's coat of arms again;
And flashing on the window pane,
Emblazoned with all its light and shade
The jovial rhymes that still remain,
Writ near a century age
By the great Major Molineaux....

Above opposite The panes of glass with the rhymes by Major Molineaux and his name scratched on them with his diamond ring, the somber clock, the coat-of-arms, the fair Princess Mary's pictured face are incredibly still there. In this same parlor, Tahitian baskets hold pink and rose carnations, white chrysanthemums, and springeri fern.

Below opposite Longfellow Chamber, with its pencil-post bed and canopy made of handwoven raw silk from New England worms, has a tall arrangement of lavender chrysanthemums, statice, and flowering branches on the lowboy.

12

13

Early in the 1920's Henry Ford restored the Wayside Inn to what was thought to be its original state, purchased nearly 5,000 acres around it, added a large dining room with a ballroom overhead, and opened it to the public. The Inn was again restored after the fire of 1955, a grant from the Ford Foundation having provided for additional research. Today the Inn is still managed by the nonprofit trust set up by Mr. Ford. Two trustees of the Wayside Inn Corporation are members of the National Trust for Historic Preservation.

Below   Arranged in a knife box in the old kitchen are chrysanthemums and cocculus leaves. Here are some of the original old boards and beams, but the ten candle sconces and ten pierced lanterns of the room have been wired for electricity. The spinning wheel and yarn winder are pushed to one side as though they might be put into use at any moment.

THE FRICK MANSION
NEW YORK, NEW YORK — 1913-1914

Below   The simplicity and restraint of the planting beds in the garden court of the Frick Mansion are well suited to the classic architecture. Azaleas and wisteria bloom in the spring, followed by other flowers in season. The Frick Collection is housed in the former residence of Henry Clay Frick, the Pittsburgh coke and steel industrialist. Built by Carrère in 1913-1914 from plans of the American architect, Thomas Hastings, the building is reminiscent of French domestic architecture of the eighteenth century. The rooms are in the style of English and French interiors of the same period.

During Mr. Frick's lifetime, the house contained the works of art he had collected over a period of forty years. He bequeathed the house and the art in trust to a Board of Trustees to provide a center for the study of art and kindred subjects. In 1935, after alterations to the building and the garden court were made by J. R. Pope, the Frick Mansion was opened to the public with a program of lectures and concerts.

BARTOW-PELL MANSION
PELHAM BAY PARK, NEW YORK — GREEK REVIVAL

The Bartow-Pell Mansion was built (1836-1842) by Robert Bartow on land orignally purchased from the Indians by his ancestor, Thomas Pell, in 1654. It is one of the finest examples of Greek Revival architecture in the country. The City of New York purchased the mansion and lands in 1888 and placed them under the jurisdiction of the Park Department. In 1914, Mrs. Charles Frederick Hoffman conceived the idea for the restoration of this grand old mansion, which was then fast falling to ruin, as headquarters for the International Garden Club, which she founded.

Below   Flowers inside and out are an important part of the decoration at the Bartow-Pell Mansion. In the drawing room, flowers designed to fill the space on the mantel under the portrait repeat the roses of the carpet. (The floors are of plain pine boards and were probably originally carpeted wall to wall.) The woodwork (probably pine or poplar, because it is easily worked) is painted and grained. The cornice is plain, but typical of classical style with crisp Grecian moldings and dentils. It was cast and shaped in molds on the wall when the plaster was wet, as was the medallion in the center of the ceiling of the adjoining room. The medallion, another classical ornamentation, is composed of Egyptian water lily and acanthus leaves, and from it hangs the chandelier. In both rooms the chandeliers have hurricane shades and cut prisms dating to the early 1800's.

Opposite   In a corner of the drawing room, lilacs and roses in an easy "S" curve repeat the flowers painted on the French porcelain vase on the piano. On a French Empire table in the center of the room, roses are used with white lilacs and Dutch irises. The piano case was probably made by Duncan Phyfe with the works by Robert and William Nunns in New York City. Most of the other furniture in the drawing room is also an American adaptation of the French Empire style.

16

Below left   On the dining table, white lilacs and Dutch iris with a few red roses for accent emphasize the white woodwork and candles. The simple though handsome mantel is of the true Roman style and has a very architectural feeling about it. The clock, an excellent example of neoclassical French Empire, is of bronze washed or plated with gilt; it is flanked by ormolu candelabra.

Below right   A romantic mass arrangement of lilacs and roses complements the painting, "Pride of the Village," by Henry Peter Grey (1814) lent by the Metropolitan Museum of Art. The furniture on which this bouquet rests, as well as the other furniture in this room, is primarily of mahogany veneer on white wood. All the acquisitions of furnishings are proper to the period and are made under the guidance of the Museum of the City of New York, the Metropolitan Museum of Art, and the Brooklyn Museum of Art.

18

TEMPE WICK HOUSE
JOCKEY HOLLOW NATIONAL PARK, NEW JERSEY — 1750

Thistles, milkweed pods, grasses, curled dock, and other field flowers provide muted color and soft texture through the winter, in the Tempe Wick House near Morristown. Henry Wick, a well-to-do-farmer, built this house in 1750, and General Arthur St. Clair occupied it in 1779-1780, while the Pennsylvania soldiers under his command camped on the adjoining hillsides. On January 1 of the following year, the troops mutinied. The story goes that to save her horse from the soldiers, Henry Wick's 21-year-old daughter Tempe hid her horse in her bedroom, hence the house was named after her.

Below The walls of the room are tulipwood stained with iron oxide. The desk is the only piece of furniture known to have been owned by Henry Wick; however the fiddleback chairs, Queen Anne gate-leg table, foot warmer, and butterfly-shelved corner cupboard might be similar to the original furniture. The plates of slipware, wood, and pewter are typical of the Revolutionary War period.

19

THE ELMS
NEWPORT, RHODE ISLAND — 1901

Below   The Elms, shown here in a front view, was modeled after the Chateau d'Asnieres, an eighteenth-century classical chateau near Paris. It was designed by Horace Trumbauer for Philadelphia coal magnate, Edward J. Berwind. Built in 1901, it is one of a number of "cottages" in Newport constructed as summer residences by wealthy industrialists around the turn of the century. The Preservation Society of Newport County purchased The Elms in 1962 to preserve an important link in the history of archichecture from Colonial times to the present.

Above opposite   The grounds of The Elms with its marble and bronze statues, playing fountains, gazebos, balustraded stables, sumptuous lawns, and sunken French gardens designed by Maservey, provide the perfect setting for the chateau. Specimen trees and shrubs from all over the world delight the eye and are properly labeled for the further enjoyment of visitors.

Below opposite   The mansion is furnished throughout with museum pieces suitable to its opulence. In the breakfast room are black and gold Chinese lacquer panels of the period of K'ang Hsi, emperor of China from 1662-1723 A.D. and noted patron of the arts. Two rococo flower arrangements suit the architectural details of this magnificent room.

21

BOSCOBEL
GARRISON-ON-HUDSON, NEW YORK — 1805

Boscobel has enlisted the help, sympathy, and appreciation of the American public, largely for its classic Adam architecture. Built at a time when good taste and good manners were the mark of a true gentleman, it continues today to be a mecca for architects and historians.

When the Westchester County Park Commission bought the mansion and its surrounding acres for a park and planned to demolish the house, Lila Acheson Wallace, who with her husband owns and directs the editorial policies of the *Reader's Digest,* gave $500,000 for the restoration. The Reader's Digest Foundation headed by Mr. and Mrs. Wallace gave another $500,000 endowment. Contributions have also been made by national and regional organizations and individuals.

The mansion was dismantled, its parts numbered, and everything stored in various places until its present 35-acre site 20 feet above the Hudson River could be acquired. During the reconstruction, completed in 1961, treasure hunts to locate the original furnishings were undertaken. Each room had mantles, doorways, ceiling medallions, and cornices designed specifically for that room:

for instance, an oval sunburst at the mantel is used again over the doors, windows, and arches.

The classic Doric columns, frieze, and pediment are softened by the unusual *Opposite* swags across the upper portico. Somehow the measurements were inaccurate, and the swags had to be recarved when the mansion was reassembled.

This view of the inside of one wing of the Orangerie at Boscobel shows *Below* masses of ferns with banks of potted geraniums, bright red wax begonias, and hanging baskets of fuchsias — all plant favorites of Colonial times.

WINTERTHUR MUSEUM

Winterthur is essentially a huge shell built to accommodate the 110 rooms collected from New Hampshire to North Carolina, either complete or as bits of woodwork, fireplaces, wallpaper, and furniture. Henry Francis du Pont began the extensive collecting of old rooms in 1927 and deeded the estate to the Winterthur Corporation in 1965. He choose the most interesting rooms he could find in America and constructed the outside to fit the inside. One room was eleven inches too wide for the alloted space so the outside walls were just moved out. As Mr. du Pont said, "Individuals and nations take their greatest inspiration through the continued remembrance of a glorious past. My purpose is to show the way early Americans lived and to preserve our country's rich tradition of craftsmanship in architecture and household arts." The rooms cover the period 1640-1840.

Below   The Chinese parlor is perhaps the most handsome room in the Winterthur Museum, which is saying much in a house which is best described in superlatives. The wallpaper painted in China in 1770 is still fresh and brilliant in color. The beautiful crystal chandelier from England, decorated with sunbursts, beads, and engraved hurricane shades, is of the same period. The

furniture is Chippendale (1750-1780). Chinese detail in the fretwork shows up under the corners of the tables by the sofa. Black and gold lacquer screens stand in the corner. White pompom chrysanthemums are shown here; when the mansion is open, flowers are placed in every room, as though the owners would be back at any moment.

The shell-top cupboard holds a tea service of Chinese export porcelain decorated in black called Jesuit. The cornices over the windows are topped with ornate carving, just one more detail that adds to the elegance of the room.

The conservatory, with masses of potted plants that can be easily replaced *Below* as different flowers come into bloom, is seen through the graceful doorway of Montmorenci, built in 1822 by General William Williams near Warrenton, North Carolina, as a gift for his third wife. Note the use of the gilt and plaster mirror and horsehair furniture typical of the period.

THE CORBIT-SHARP HOUSE
ODESSA, DELAWARE — 1772-1774

Opposite　　The formal garden of this eighteenth-century Georgian house built by William Corbit was designed in 1942 by H. Rodney Sharp. The geometric, germander-bordered beds are filled with herbs and flowers. Tulips are featured in the spring, chrysanthemums in the fall. Flowering shrubs and fruit trees are on either side of the formal gardens. This house, restored and endowed by Mr. Sharp, is administered by the Henry Francis du Pont Winterthur Museum.

Below　　The drawing room is furnished with Queen Anne and Chippendale pieces. At the fireplace are a Philadelphia Queen Anne easy chair with trifid foot and a New York Chippendale chair (c. 1760). The woodwork is a gray blue, and the plaster walls are a light salmon pink. Over the mantel is a painting presumed to be by William Williams, a mid-eighteenth-century artist. The chimney breast with its crown of broken-pitch pediment is flanked by fluted pilasters. Roses in a mass dominate the piano.

26

STEPHEN HOPKINS HOUSE
STEPHEN, RHODE ISLAND

Stephen Hopkins was Chief Justice of the Superior Court, Governor of Rhode Island ten times, a signer of the Declaration of Independence, and holder of many other public offices. In 1927, when this modest house of an illustrious American was about to be demolished, the National Society of Colonial Dames of America in the State of Rhode Island and Providence Plantations had it moved to its present site and carefully restored it. Two rooms date to 1707; additions were made in 1743.

Below   In the parlor, peonies and mock orange in a plain bowl grace the gate-leg table. The fireplace is framed by bolection molding. Above it are round-topped panels which flank a fine shell cupboard, a distinctive Rhode Island feature. The hearth is made of bricks brought over as ballast in ships. The simple Queen Anne chairs and mirror seem much at home in this room.

The keeping room of early days was the center of family life, combining the functions of living room, dining room, kitchen, and, often, bedroom. In this homely setting are simple arrangements of fragrant nodding cabbage roses (*Rosa centifolia*) adorning the tavern table and steeplebush (*Spiraea tomentosa*) with blueberries (*Vaccinium*) massed on the stand by the fireplace. The counting desk has a lovely fan motif. Note the ladder-back and banister-back chairs. Two foot warmers are on the hearth below the crane in the fireplace.

Below

PHILADELPHIA MUSEUM OF FINE ARTS
PHILADELPHIA, PENNSYLVANIA

Peking Palace Room — Chinese Seventeenth Century

Below   Herbaceous peonies and pine branches are arranged in Chinese vases by a member of the Garden Club of America in a room from a palace in Peking (1622-1627) restored at the Philadelphia Museum of Fine Arts. Peonies, described as the national flower of China, have been associated for centuries with aristocracy, beauty and grandeur in poetry and legend. Pine branches too have had a persistent symbolism in the Orient, where they represent long life, old age and winter. Since the art of China, like that of Japan, is based on using three main lines to represent the heaven-man-earth philosophy, the plant materials are appropriately composed here to form the outline of a scalene triangle.

Abbey in the Pyrenees — French Eleventh Century

Opposite   The Romanesque Cloisters are from the Abbey of Saint-Genis-Fontaines built in 1086 in the Pyrenees. The arrangement of potted plants by Mrs. Horace Jones of the Garden Club of America was done mostly in white flowers to keep it authentic to the period for which it was designed. The trees include

lemon and orange, acanthus, fig, cedar of Lebanon, *Laurus nobilis,* and *Cinnamomum zeylanicum.* Old-fashioned thorny white roses, Madonna lilies, artichokes, *Primula veris,* marguerites, violas, violets, sempervivums, wild strawberries, and such herbs as santolina, lavender, thyme and artemisia were also used.

French Chapel—Gothic Fifteenth Century

Below   Miss Emily Bache and other members of the Garden Club of America arranged a flower carpet in the French Gothic Chapel (c. 1400) using great quantities of rose petals in varied colors, as well as tulips, mimosa, and lilacs with a border of leaves of ilex and boxwood.

CASA AMESTI
MONTEREY, CALIFORNIA — 1830-1846

Below   Casa Amesti, a two-story adobe structure, was erected by Don Jose Amesti in the 1830's. The house was enlarged and balconies added to the street and patio in 1845. Don Jose gave the house to his daughter Carmen when she married a Scotch sailor Don Santiago (born James McKinley) who became a naturalized Mexican. The house remained in the Amesti family until 1912 and was acquired by Mrs. Frances Adler Elkins six years later. She restored the cool old thick-walled building and used it to house her remarkable collection of Oriental and other art, embellishing the building inside and out in a manner that equips it for contemporary living, with the advice of her brother, David Adler, FAIA, the late Chicago architect. The garden is distinctly Mediterranean in feeling — clipped box hedges and columnar yews softened by the natural forms of lemon, fig, and palm trees.

In 1935, Mrs. Elkins bequeathed Casa Amesti to the National Trust and at the present time it is maintained and operated for the Trust by the Old Capitol Club of Monterey.

ROSEDOWN

ST. FRANCISVILLE, LOUISIANA — 1835

Rosedown was built in 1835 by a wealthy young planter, Daniel Turnbull, for his wife, Martha. A perfectionist with rare artistic perception, Daniel created a stately house and filled it with treasures from the capitals of Europe. The riverboats which carried his bountiful cotton crops to New Orleans returned with elegant silver, chandeliers, and especially made furniture. In Italy, he and Martha selected marble statuary to be placed in their formal gardens.

Like their friends and relatives in the Felicianas, the young Turnbulls enjoyed the pleasures of landed gentry — gay parties, cards, musicals, hunting to hounds, and horse racing. When war came, the grandeur of Rosedown, like that of other mansions around them, diminished and then disappeared.

In the spring of 1956, Mr. and Mrs. Milton Underwood of Houston, Texas, inspired by the beautiful camellias and azaleas in the gardens, purchased the plantation and restored it as it was when the Turnbulls first built it. In 1964, they opened Rosedown to the public as a living museum of the Old South.

Opposite   In the dining room, bowls of red and yellow roses grace the mahogany table. The chairs, also mahogany, are Duncan Phyfe originals with haircloth seats. At the far end of the room, the mirror over the black and gold Carrara marble mantel reflects one of the two Sully portraits of the Turnbulls. The four-tier half-round table (c. 1800) is French, as is the crystal and bronze candle sconce (c. 1835) above it. The table is set with Chamberlain Worcester dinner service, Baccarat crystal, and English Georgian silverware and accessories. On the left, a marble top mahogany serving table with mirror back reflects the Louis Philippe Aubusson rug (c. 1830-1848). Overhead is a needlework punkah (used to fan the room) on its original frame.

Following page   Matched spring bouquets including Easter lilies, camellias, and calendulas pick up the golds in the tapestry carpet and elsewhere in the lovely music room. At right, a Regency armchair (c. 1815) covered in antique French brocade and a cane-back Regency chair (c. 1800) flank a carved gilded table with a floral painted top, ormolu mounted tree trunk, and rockery base (c. 1820). At the fireplace, an antique fan-shaped brass fire screen conceals the hearth. The Carrara marble mantel supports a gilt bronze Louis XV clock (c. 1800) with two figures representing America. (There is a similar clock in the Metropolitan Museum of Art in New York.) Above it is a Regency convex mirror (c. 1800); the wallpaper border is a copy of a French Empire design (c. 1810). The antique French lampas draperies (c. 1850) with their elaborate

34

lambrequins serve as backdrop for a Regency sofa with antique needlepoint pillows (c. 1850). The Italian console with Blackamoor at left has a *rouge flandre* marble top. In the foreground is a harp made by Browne and Bockwell in the early nineteenth century. A six light crystal chandelier made in England (c. 1830) illuminates the room.

WOODLAWN PLANTATION
MOUNT VERNON, VIRGINIA — GEORGIAN

Woodlawn Plantation, once part of George Washington's Mount Vernon estate, was his wedding gift to Nelly Custis, Martha Washington's granddaughter, when she married Washington's nephew, Lawrence Lewis, in 1799. The gift included 2000 acres of the Mount Vernon estate, a mill, and a distillery. The mansion itself was designed by William Thornton, first architect of the nation's Capitol; its bricks were burned on the place, and local Acquia stone trims the exterior.

The Woodlawn Public Foundation purchased the mansion in 1948 and nine years later turned it over to the National Trust for Historic Preservation, under whose direction it was restored, furnished, and opened to the public.

Below

Roads, paths, and flower beds have been replaced by the Garden Club of Virginia, following records and archaelogical evidence. Two rose parterres have been copied, one from Mount Vernon, the other from Tudor Place. The circle of boxwood near the west entrance (shown) was probably "slipped" from shrubs at Mount Vernon.

Opposite

A mixed summer bouquet beside a wine decanter enlivens the Queen Anne table in the music room. The woodwork is handsomely detailed, and the graining on the doors, fashionable in that day, has been restored.

LOW HOUSE
SAVANNAH, GEORGIA — VICTORIAN 1848

It was from this handsome house that Juliette Gordon Low, widow of the son of the builder, organized the first Girl Scout troup in America. In 1928, the home was bought by the National Society of the Colonial Dames of America in Georgia as their headquarters, and most of its furnishings, which are in keeping with the style of the house, have been given by members and friends of this society.

Below At Christmas one year, the doors in the entrance hall were festooned with garlands of native pine and boxwood. Just inside the door was a kissing ball made of mistletoe and green velvet bows. The English Sheraton mahogany breakfast table in the foreground had as its centerpiece a hurricane globe with an artistic arrangement of fresh apples, grapes, and other fruits. The sofa opposite it is in the style of Sheraton. The portraits are of Mr. and Mrs. William Taylor and Anne Graham, and the Oriental rugs are primarily red and blue. Regency chairs are on either side of the mahogany Hepplewhite card table in the background.

Opposite In the well-proportioned dining room with its decorated plaster cornice copied from an Italian design, a gold-leaf Victorian mirror over a marble mantel re-

flects an arrangement of several varieties of white camellias used with podocarpus. A Sheraton mahogany dining table with two pedestals (c. 1790) holds a centerpiece of fresh green grapes, lemons, plums, raisins, nuts, and sweetmeats in a gold-washed epergne with crystal bowls. The matching compotes filled with fruits and nuts and the wide bands of gold velvet ribbon create an elegance well suited to the architecture of this dignified house. The crystal chandelier was made in England about 1810. Chippendale-style chairs have needlepoint seats of Georgia birds and flowers worked by members of the Georgia Colonial Dames.

Below   Double drawing rooms share a garland of native pine and boxwood entwined with red ribbon. In the foreground is a fine New York settee with a design of swags and tassels carved on the back. The garlanded portrait over the mantel is of Mrs. Joseph J. Wilder, second president of the Georgia Dames. Red camellias are on the black marble mantel below the portrait. Of special interest in the back drawing room is a pair of carved rosewood mèridiennes (French Empire sofas) with matching footstools. The native pine Christmas tree is decorated in the manner of the middle 1800's with candy canes, cookies, cornucopias, and tiny wrapped packages.

BRUSH-EVERARD HOUSE
WILLIAMSBURG, VIRGINIA — 1717

John Brush, gunsmith and armorer, built this house in 1717, and eventually it came into the hands of Thomas Everard, a wealthy tobacco planter elected mayor of Williamsburg in 1766. Mr. Everard remodeled and enlarged the house and laid out the gardens.

Below   The mass arrangement made by Miss Edna Pennell for the entrance hall includes gladioli, lilies, bee balm, daisies, and hollyhocks. Two Chippendale chairs flank the table against the dado. Note the random-width planking in the floor.

The framed quillwork, so called for its elaborate composition of painted and gilded rolled paper quills, also contains shells, mica, and wax figures. School girls made such decorations as part of their education as evidenced by this advertisement from the Boston *Gazette* of May 26, 1775: "This is to give notice, That Mrs. Hiller still continues to Keep School in Hanover-Street . . . where young Ladies may be taught Wax work, Transparent and Filligree, painting on Glass, Quill work and Feather work, Japanning, Embroidering with Silver and Gold, Tentstitch. . . ."

Below   In the dining room, green silk moire striped with red and gold is used at the window. It suggests the opulence in which a gentleman of the period lived. Queen Anne chairs are upholstered in the same fabric. On the table with satin ribbons, a cone — it could be made of wood or styrofoam — holds fresh limes and boxwood clippings, providing a touch of tailored elegance.

GOVERNOR'S PALACE
WILLIAMSBURG, VIRGINIA — c. 1720

In 1926, Mr. John D. Rockefeller, Jr. became interested in the restoration of Williamsburg "to re-create accurately the environment of the men and women of eighteenth-cenutry Williamsburg and to bring about such an understanding of their lives and times that present and future generations may more vividly appreciate the contributions of these early Americans to the ideals and culture of our country."

This residence, occupied by the Royal Governors of Virginia in the eighteenth century, had been burned in 1782 and reconstruction was begun in 1930 following a floor plan made by Thomas Jefferson.

In the large mass arrangement in the little dining room are maple leaves pressed to hold their shape and color; dock gathered through the summer as it changes to pale green, pink, light tan, and dark brown; artemisia; yellow yarrow; and lunaria (only the center membrane is used after the "money-in-both pockets," as the French say, has been peeled away and the tiny moons are revealed).

Below   The dropleaf table (c. 1740) has shell carving, beloved of eightenth-century cabinetmakers, both on the walnut underframing and on the mahogany legs which end in ball feet. The top is also mahogany.

45

Below In the small parlor leading from the entrance hall, a portrait of Evelyn Bird hangs above an antique white and brown marble mantel on which are five pairs of Chelsea porcelain birds. The tilt-top tea table with scalloped edge is japanned in black and gold. The walnut armchair with a winged satyr's mask carved on the front (c. 1725) is covered with needlework. The settee and side chairs are covered with gold damask. The chandelier is early English. The cut glass candleholders with hanging lusters and engraved shades are Waterford. In this elegant setting an arrangement of brilliant jonquils is displayed in a Chinese ginger jar.

Opposite Wreathes of box and bayberry decorate a wall of the family dining room. Miss Edna Pennell uses a simple arrangement of apples and magnolia leaves

on the mantel above the marble fireplace with its classical acanthus leaf decoration. The portrait by Charles Bridges is of Alexander Spotswood. Of the seven governors who lived at the Palace, he contributed most to the laying out of the gardens, even offering to pay for them himself if the Council of Burgesses thought them too expensive.

Pineapples for hospitality and apples for good health marked the Christmas season one year in the formal dining room of the Governor's Palace. A wooden cone with projecting nails held the fruit in place. Small pieces of balsam for fragrance were tucked between the apples and around the base. Walnuts were scattered around the lower part.

Following page top

47

The four silver candlesticks, like fluted Corinthian colunms, were made in England in 1741 by John Robertson. Candlelight and fruit reflect in the polished mahogany top of the mid-eigtheenth-century dining table making it easy to imagine a festive atmosphere. A set of George II English chairs with their elaborate carving and pierced splat have covered needlepoint seats worked in the flame stitch, so characteristic of the period. Silver sconces (originally from Keele Hall, Staffordshire, England) with the cipher of William and Mary illuminate the walls.

Below opposite Massed-line bouquets of fresh flowers arranged by Miss Edna Pennell adorn a bedroom in the Governor's Palace. Blue and white Dutch tiles line the fireplace; a china dog guards the hearth. The tilt-top tea table (c. 1775) has a top of Pontypool japanned sheet-iron with pierced edge and polychrome and gilt decorations on a black ground. The tripod pedestal is of japanned beech. The bed and hangings are Jacobean.

Pressed Flower Pictures Pressed flower pictures are just as popular in Colonial Williamsburg today as they were when the Colonial ladies made them.

Pick flowers and leaves at their peak of bloom and when there is no dew on them. Lay them flat between several layers of newspaper. Add weights (books or bricks) and set in a warm dry place; the plant material will be dry in one to two weeks. Flowers that have small calyxes are easily pressed flat. Florets of such flowers as the delphinium may be pressed individually and reassembled on the picture mat. Small-scaled foliages, garden flowers, and weeds are all useful for pressed flower pictures.

Once dry, arrange the flowers and leaves on the sturdy mat of a picture frame. Silk, velvet, and other fabrics can be used as a covering over the mat. Embroidery wools wound around the mat and construction paper are also satisfactory as backgrounds. When the flowers are pleasingly arranged, you can add a tiny dab of cement on the back of each and replace them in the design or you can leave them in position without cementing. Lay the glass-fitted frame carefully over the flower picture and carefully turn everything over. Poke tiny brads into the reverse side of the frame to hold everything in place. Conceal backing with heavy craft paper cut to fit, then pasted onto the frame. Hang the pictures from concealed wire or use decorative velvet ribbon.

In designing the pictures, you may simulate containers by cutting out solid leaves, or you may use leaves to simulate roots. Overlap the plant materials to give depth and body to the design.

These pressed flower pictures are from the Williamsburg collection at B. Altman & Co. Commercial pressed-flowers are often colored artificially, but most flower-picture designers prefer the more subtle natural colors and are willing to redo the pictures every few years if necessary.

48

49

GEORGE WYTHE HOUSE
WILLIAMSBURG, VIRGINIA — 1754-1789

The house has been refurnished with things suitable to the period when George Wythe lived there and ran an estate plantation in miniature. He was a law professor at the College of William and Mary, a member of the House of Burgresses, and a signer of the Declaration of Independence. The design of the austere symmetrically balanced house is credited to Wythe's father-in-law, Richard Taliaferro. It is actually a small plantation with the gardens and out buildings.

Below   On the mantel in a bedroom are two arrangements of tiny dried flowers in delft bricks done by Miss Edna Pennell. On the window seat, magnolia leaves are used with flowering fruit tree branches. The chest-on-chest with fluted pilasters, ogee bracket feet, and domed top was possibly made in Connecticut during the last quarter of the 1700's.

Opposite   Green royal and cinnamon fern fronds and beech leaves, carefully pressed and dried to hold their shape and color, form a lacy background for the boneset, grasses, wheat, dark thermopsis seed pods, yellow and rust strawflowers, and pale green hydrangeas used in a mass arrangement executed by the late Louise Fisher. The mahogany and fruitwood piano was made by Beck of London, England, in 1785.

SCHUYLER-HAMILTON HOUSE

In December, 1779, Washington's army of more than 10,000 men camped at Morristown. The general himself and his official family including his capable twenty-three-year-old secretary, Alexander Hamilton, lived at Ford Mansion. The chief physician and surgeon of the Continental army, Dr. John Cochran, stayed a quarter mile from headquarters at the home of Dr. John Campfield.

Since the hills of Morris County were a natural fortress, many of the officers brought their wives to this comparatively safe place. Martha Washington arrived that December, and Dr. Cochran's wife, the only sister of General Philip Schuyler of Albany, journeyed here to be with her husband. That same winter, dark-eyed Miss Elizabeth Schuyler, daughter of the general, visited her aunt at Campfield House. The dashing young Hamilton, having known Betsy in Albany, renewed the acquaintance, and with the blooming of spring they announced their betrothal. Mrs. Hamilton was a devoted wife, and when she died at the age of ninety-seven she still wore around her neck a tiny silk bag containing one of Hamilton's letters written to her that difficult yet exciting winter.

To commemorate this charming wartime romance, the Campfield House was renamed the Schuyler-Hamilton House when it was purchased by the Morristown Chapter of the Daughters of the American Revolution. In 1964, the Home Garden Club of Morristown planted a Colonial garden of flowers and culinary and medicinal herbs on the site of Dr. Campfield's original garden.

Opposite   On the Governor Winthrop maple desk in the parlor beside a minature of Dr. Cochran is an arrangement of field flowers in an ironstone mold. Bristly woundwort, bugloss, lavender Monarda, meadow rue, and Queen Anne's lace arranged by the author add a frothy note to the otherwise utilitarian desk with the brass-studded leather box, sand shaker, eye glasses, candle snuffer, and inkwell.

WILLIAM BLOUNT MANSION
KNOXVILLLE, TENNESSEE — 1792

Below   The William Blount Mansion, with its separate office in back, was the first frame building west of the Allegheny Mountains; it was built from lumber which had to come overland or by flatboat. Blount, made governor of the territory south of the Ohio River by President Washington in 1790, succeeded in negotiating the Treaty of Holston with forty-one of the principal Cherokee chiefs in 1791, thus giving settlers relief from Indian attacks and leading to the founding of the city of Knoxville. Under Blount's leadership Tennessee was admitted to the union on June 1, 1796. The Mansion was designated a Registered National Historic Landmark in 1965. Its gardens are maintained by the Knoxville Garden Club.

Opposite   In the dining room, the corner cupboard was finished with buttermilk paint and sand, which kept the color diffused. The Chinese porcelain, made some 350 years ago, is "bat" or "pomegranate" in design. The chairs are English Chippendale, and the table is a "country" Hepplewhite probably of American manufacture.

The arrangements on the table feature the pineapple, long a symbol of hospitality and plenty. Even in pagan days, fruits were used decoratively for harvest festivals. In the fifteenth century, della Robbia wreaths were adorned with enameled fruits. During the Renaissance, fruit was used in great mass arrangements to express the cycle of the seasons. The tradition of expressing bounty with fruit and vegetable forms continued in gracious Colonial days and is still practiced today.

55

VAN CORTLANDT MANOR
CROTON-ON-HUDSON, NEW YORK — 1749-1814

The original stone core of the Manor House is presumed to have existed when Stephanus van Cortlandt bought this large tract of land north of Croton. Van Cortlandt's descendents occupied the house for more than 200 years, then it was acquired by Mr. John D. Rockefeller in 1953 and restored to the period of 1749-1814. Van Cortlandt Manor was opened to the public by Sleepy Hollow Restorations in 1959. The house is constructed of red field stone, its lower windows surrounded by yellow Dutch brick. The raised porch, which is most often associated with the architecture of the American South, may be unique in the Hudson Valley.

Opposite   On a marble-topped serving table, also in the dining room, is a pyramid of fruit and nuts in eighteenth-century style. The looking glass is transitional Queen Anne to Chippendale style (mid-eighteenth century), probaby New York. It is pine and poplar painted black with gesso and gilt.

Below   The dining room has putty colored walls and cupboards with Dutch red interiors. The William and Mary dining room table with mahogany top and cherry base (c. 1700) was made in New York as were the six New York Chippendale chairs. Although it was known that the chairs originally in the room were made by the Goddard family in Newport, Rhode Island, these were not available at the time of the restoration. Chinese export porcelain and Canton ware which belonged to the Van Cortlandts may be seen in the cupboard. The curtains are made from a reproduction of a piece of eighteenth-century bourette in the flame pattern; the rug is a bright Ushak. The tables are set as they might have been for a New Year's Day visit in the eighteenth century. Berried branches of holly are in the porcelain bowl on the table at left. The dining table holds a fruit and ivy centerpiece, with a wine decanter and freshly baked cake garnished with holly.

THE WHITE HOUSE
WASHINGTON, D.C.

Opposite   The garden looking from the President's office toward the Executive office is called the Rose Garden, but in springtime the border is resplendent with tulips, forget-me-nots, and grape-hyacinths (*Muscari*) below the crab apple trees. President Truman added the balcony on the South Portico in 1946 to replace awnings which marred the grace of the columns.

Below   After the fire of 1814 destroyed the furnishings of this beautifully proportioned oval room, President Monroe ordered the Empire furniture and bronzes shown here. Two-toned cream satin covers the walls below a draped blue valance edged in a purple tasseled Empire border. Of the same blue are the upholstery, table cover, and portions of the carpet. Displayed together for the first time on the walls of the Blue Room are the portraits of the first seven Presidents of the United States. The French cabinetmaker Pierre-Antonie Bellange built the gilt pier table and the side chairs; his name is stamped on the bottom of the front rails. The bust of Washington under his portrait is by the Italian sculptor Ceracchi. Two flower arrangements are shown on the table in the center of the room. In a Chinese porcelain bowl are iris, stock, carnations,

Below left   and Shasta daisies. In a view from the other end of the room, heather; white, pink, and salmon gerbera; blue iris; white marguerite; and white, beige, and yellow single chrysanthemums are arranged in a vermeil bowl.

Below right   The Fine Arts Committee under Mrs. John F. Kennedy restored the Green Room as a Federal parlor of the late eighteenth or early nineteenth century. Moss green silk moire covers the walls, and on the floor is an Axminster rug. Mahogany and satinwood settees of New England origin covered in embroidered cotton flank the fireplace. On either side of the table, lattice-backed mahogany side chairs, attributed to Samuel McIntire of Salem, Massachusetts, are silhouetted against the dado. On the tables beside the fireplace are flowered porcelain pitchers made by the firm of Benjamin Tucker in Philadelphia, probably after 1828. The "Hannibal clock" of bronze doré on the marble mantel was imported by President Monroe in 1817. The famous portrait of Benjamin Franklin reading a document near the bust of Isaac Newton was painted by the Scottish artist David Martin in London in 1767. A small arrangement of all-white flowers in a Chinese export porcelain mug is on the candlestand between the sofa and the racquet-back armchair. Against the far wall on a mahogany inlaid card table (c. 1800) is a large mass arrangement of white, yellow, and bronze flowers.

Another corner of the Green Room features a mahogany secretary made in 1797 by the noted Annapolis cabinetmaker, John Shaw. Before the desk is an upholstered Sheraton tub chair, and in the background is a Martha Washington armchair dating from the early nineteenth century. On the lid of the secretary are a green glass and gilt bronze inkwell (probably of French origin), an early nineteenth-century brass candlestick, and a Chinese export mug (1770-1790) holding salmon and white geraniums, bouvardia, stevia, and hawthorne berries. Behind the glass doors are a Tucker porcelain pitcher made in Philadelphia around 1828 and a rare footed plate of Chinese export porcelain made for the American market and decorated as a memorial to President Washington.

Below left

Each spring, the First Lady entertains the Senate ladies at the White House. A luncheon given by Mrs. Lyndon B. Johnson featured china from a different administration on each table. This one shows pieces from the Woodrow Wilson collection. The flowers were yellow and white marguerites, gypsophila, lily of the valley, beige miniature carnations, white ranunculus, and anemones in shades of purple arranged in a pierced fruit compote of French porcelain marked "H & Co." The menu: Prosciutto and melon, Supreme of chicken Maryland, Purée Favorite, Fresh fruit au Cointreau, and Demi-tasse.

Below right

LOWELL DAMON HOUSE
WAUWATOSA, WISCONSIN — NEW ENGLAND COLONIAL

The Lowell Damon House was started in 1844 by Oliver Damon and finished in 1846 by his son, Lowell, using the surrounding forests for lumber, fieldstones for the foundations, and burning their own bricks. It passed through various families and was in danger of being torn down in 1939 when it was purchased by Alexander Rogers, who had lived in the house as a child. He deeded it to the Milwaukee County Historical Society in 1941. The restoration of the house, garden, and furnishings was a real community project led by the garden clubs with the residents providing a great deal of hard work and funds.

Below   Bronze peony foliage and chrysanthemums harmonize with the warm tones of the walnut wooden pegged table. The Seth Thomas grandfather clock has wooden works in a mahogany case with a painted wooden face. The pictures are probably lithographs on paper mounted on cloth of known portraits of Martha and George Washington. The black Boston rocker has its original stenciling and painted flower designs. The small Early Victorian rocker is of tiger

maple. The wallpaper is a print typical of the period. Note the shadow on the wall of an old kerosene lamp that has been wired for electricity.

This maple rope bed in a bedroom has a rose pattern coverlet woven in New York State. The container of the massed line arrangement on the cherry sewing table is a Chelsea ware teapot with blue luster raised figures. Above it hangs a gold leaf mirror. The wallpaper is a document print, and the flooring is the original wide pine boards.   *Below*

MUSEUM OF FINE ARTS
BOSTON, MASSACHUSETTS

West Boxford Room — Early American

Below   Members of the Massachusetts Federation of Garden Clubs have festooned this room, originally from West Boxford, Massachusetts, for Christmas. A garland of box and yew trimmed with crab apples graces the fireplace, with its teapot and kettle and the cradle nearby. Below the portrait, painted in Boston in 1687, is an arrangement in a pewter trencher of pink geraniums such as

a Colonial housewife might have tended all winter in a sunny window. The tiered holly and crab-apple centerpiece on the gate-leg table (1670-1700) — oak like the other furniture — is made from two pewter plates separated by an inverted pewter cup. The table is set with pewter mugs, bone-handled pewter knives and forks, and pewter porringers on wooden plates. Mrs. Hollis Gray, Mrs. Howard Spicker, and Mrs. Donald Wyman made the arrangements.

Essex County Room — c. 1700

Aganist the mellow pine paneling of a room from Essex County, Massa-chusetts, reconstructed at the Musem of Fine Arts in Boston, Mrs. Raymond Cronin, Mrs. C. L. Hauthaway, and Mrs. Edward Robertson, members of the Massachusetts Federation of Garden Clubs, have placed Christmas decorations. Traditional holly, boxwood, and red roses in a tole epergne are on the table to the left. In front of the window, pine and a single rosette of dried mullein leaves, like a great furry rose of pale gold, are used in a pewter container.

Below

A wreath of evergreens above the chair to the right of the window balances the tall clock with its engaged spiral columns. On the desk (right) in a Stafford-shire container is a mass of artemisia, andromeda, and juniper with gray berries, probably bay berries, all things that would have been available in the period between 1700 and 1730 when the furniture was built in this country.

George Shepard House—c. 1803

Below   The drawing room from a house built by George Shepard in Bath, Maine, is now in the Museum of Fine Arts in Boston. Taking the elaborately carved mantels of Samuel McIntire, of the same period, as her inspiration, Mrs. Anson Howe Smith has simulated them with dried plant material. Using pellon tinted to match the mantel as the base, she made a basket of dried pampas grass, flowers from ginko leaves or artichoke scales with tansy blossom centers. The grapes are oak galls, round lumps formed by the tree when an insect egg is laid in a branch or leaf. The center medallion is edged with tansy blooms alternated with split peas; similar decorations are on the end panels.

To harmonize with the green and orange-red in the wallpaper, she used evergreens and pyracantha berries on the side table (left). The Hepplewhite and Sheraton-style furniture is in keeping with the elegance of the room and the period.

66

OLD SALEM

WINSTON-SALEM, NORTH CAROLINA — SOUTHERN

This is one of fifteen rooms from Southern homes (1690-1820) in the Museum of Early Decorative Arts, owned and operated by Old Salem, Inc., the nonprofit corporation that exhibits the Moravin Congregation Town restoration. The room is from the small home of a planter in Edgecomb County, North Carolina.

Below left

Dried hydrangeas, honesty, rabbit tobacco, strawflowers, goldenrod, false dragonhead, Nandina berries, and swamp grass are arranged in a polychrome decorated delftware bowl (c. 1760). The corner table is Queen Anne from Virginia or North Carolina (c. 1750).

Below right

In the same room, a pair of Bristol delftware crocus bricks (c. 1750) holding strawflowers, statice, and heather flank a spice cabinet on a walnut Chippendale table from Virginia (c. 1770-80). The large portrait is of Richard Sprigg of Strawberry Hill, Maryland, painted in 1761 by John Hesselius; the smaller prints are mezzotints of Generals George Washington and Charles Lee.

VISCAYA
MIAMI, FLORIDA

One thousand masons, carpenters, artists, and metal craftsmen worked for five years to create this Renaissance palace-fortress built by James Deering, co-founder of International Harvester in 1916. He had begun collecting art treasures some twenty years before its construction — a Roman bath discovered in the ruins of Pompeii, the interior of a chateau, and priceless treasures which had been owned by queens — storing his acquisitions to await the building of Viscaya Palace, now operated by the Metropolitan Dade County Park and Recreation Department.

Below   An aerial view shows the house built around a court, with ten acres of formal gardens displayed among thirty acres of what was once mangrove jungle.

Opposite   In this view from the south terrace, one can see jasmine parterres, bougainvillea on the roof of the gazebo, blue allamanda beside the statue, and oleander in the pot to the right of the statue.

SEWARD HOUSE
AUBURN, NEW YORK — 1816-1817

William Henry Seward was the first Whig governor of New York State, serving two terms (1839-43). He was the acknowledged leader of the anti-slavery group in the Senate and a brilliant Secretary of State in the Cabinets of Presidents Lincoln and Johnson. Seward was a leading figure in the purchase of Alaska and a founder of the Republican Party.

Married to Frances Miller, daughter of his law partner, he had moved into his father-in-law's house in 1824. This same house was left by a descendent, William H. Seward III, upon his death in 1952, as a memorial to his father and grandfather. The house is administered by the Foundation Historical Association, Inc. of Auburn, which spent four years in restoring its original furnishings.

Below   Blue salvia, asters, nasturtiums, zinnias, and snapdragons from the Seward gardens are arranged in the small epergne on the ninety-five-year-old Steinway grand piano in the drawing room. The painting in the background is *Letchworth Park* by Thomas Cole.

Opposite   On the mantel in the dining room is a graceful arrangement of ivy and gladioli. The ivy was originally given to Seward by Washington Irving who brought it from the home of Sir Walter Scott. The gladioli colors — white, pale yellow, rose, and red — contrast and harmonize with the rich red Victorian wall covering and relate to the colors in the Chinese porcelain.

MORVEN

PRINCETON, NEW JERSEY—GEORGIAN AND GREEK REVIVAL 1701

When Richard Stockton, a Quaker, came from New Amsterdam in 1691, he bought 6,000 acres from William Penn. The land on which Morven stands was part of this purchase and was held by the Stockton family until 1945 when Governor Walter E. Edge presented the house, beautifully restored, to the people of New Jersey as the Governor's Mansion.

Now on Stockton Street and Library Place in the charming university town of Princeton, the house was on a road which later became the Old Dutch Trail, then the Kings Highway. Cornwallis, in pursuit of Washington in 1776, made his headquarters here and did great damage to the house, digging up the garden where he found and appropriated two of the three chests the Stocktons had buried there.

Richard Stockton, a signer of the Declaration of Independence, was imprisoned as a traitor by the British. Later he renounced his allegiance to the new colonies in order to go back to Princeton. History has forgiven Stockton in the light of the subsequent American victories and the assistance rendered the new country by the Stockton family.

Above opposite Mrs. John C. Bayles has arranged roses, anemones, daffodils, tulips, flowering cherry, grape hyacinths, and graceful vine tendrils in twin urns on the library mantel. This portrait of Mrs. Mary Field Stockton, wife of Richard Stockton, Jr., was painted about 1810 by Charles B. Lawrence.

Below opposite A silver bowl on the dining table holds snapdragons, carnations, roses and chrysanthemums, arranged by Mrs. F. A. Berrall.

Following page Airy sprays of orchids, gladioli, tulips and angelwing begonia leaves arranged by a member of the Garden Club of New Jersey contrast pleasingly with the gold damask walls at Morven. All of the photographs are by Mrs. Bayles.

72

74

BELLINGRATH GARDENS AND HOME
THEODORE, ALABAMA

Bellingrath Gardens began as a fishing lodge for Walter D. and Bessie Morse Bellingrath, and it was in the surrounding woods that Mrs. Bellingrath first planted azaleas. Her success was so marked that the Bellingraths soon decided to create a "wondrous garden" from the forest. In 1927, a trip to Europe inspired them to call in professional landscape architects and, under the direction of George B. Rogers, the major transformation was begun. Today, the Bellingrath Gardens are famous for their outstanding collections of azaleas, dogwood trees, roses, hydrangeas, camellias, magnolias, and sweet jasmine. Each season, each week, brings its wealth of bloom. Mr. Bellingrath was fond of comparing his gardens to a lovely lady with fifty-two gowns, one for each week of the year. According to the will of Mr. Bellingrath (he died in 1955), six trustees of the Bellingrath-Morse Foundation are empowered to perpetuate the magnificent estate so "that those who come after us may visit the Gardens and enjoy them."

Below   The house itself is of handmade brick and wrought-iron lace work, all more than a century old. Its architect described it as "a mingling of the French, Eng-

lish and Mediterranean influences, while the interior presents a blend of décor embracing chiefly the English Renaissance and Colonial America." Victorian influences are evident in many of the antiques left for future generations to enjoy. The furniture, Old English silver, and rare eighteenth- and nineteenth-century objects of art include Meissen, Sévres, and English porcelains and nine complete dinner services collected by the mistress of the house.

Below   Against the brick wall in the porch dining room are hung remarkably detailed needlepoint portraits of Generals Washington, Lee, and Jackson. On the table, a predominantly white flower arrangement echoes the white of the doorway arches.

Above opposite   In the dining room are an English Chippendale dining table and chairs once owned by Sir Thomas Lipton. The Meissen centerpiece holds roses that repeat the red in draperies, rug, and chairs.

Below opposite   Man's love for plant life goes back to the beginning of history, and it would be impossible to find an art form in which flowers have not been a source of inspiration. Here a fine porcelain Meissen urn with cover is shown. It is profusely decorated with boldly modeled naturalistic applied flowers, the cupid and other figurines making a minor accent. The base is typical of nineteenth-century revivals of earlier Meissen ware.

THOMAS COOKE HOUSE
EDGARTON, MASSACHUSETTS — 1765-1766

Shipbuilders constructed this house in 1765, giving it cambered beams bowed in the middle like those of a ship; as a result, there is a distinct slant to the floors and ceilings. The house, built for Thomas Cooke, collector of customs and justice of the peace, is one of three of this kind known to exist on the eastern seaboard. Outside the kitchen door, the herb garden has been *Below* carefully restored by the Duke County Historical Society. Thyme, basil, parsley, rue, rosemary, borage, feverfew, mint, sage, dill, celeriac, and tansy grow just as they did when Thomas Cooke lived there.

Dahlias arranged in a Parian ware vase brought from England in 1860 stand *Opposite* on a nest of tea tables brought from China. The banister-back chair, made in 1600, was owned by James Allen. Note how carefully the paneling has been designed to slope from left down to the right so it conforms to the slant of the ceiling and floor.

With the developing enthusiasm for collecting antique furniture, it is logical to expect also a revival of interest in antique skills, and this has indeed occurred. Almost forgotten crafts—crewel embroidery, quilting, bead flower work, framing of pressed flowers, and the making of shell ornaments — are all back in fashion again as heritages of our earlier history.

Opposite This shell wreath was made in 1870 by Mrs. Mary A. Edson, probably during a long winter while awaiting her husband's return from a whaling voyage. A glass-covered circular shadow box with a frame appears to be the background to which were secured small shells and flowers made from shells. Such cases can be bought or made to any measurement and painted any desired color.

The shells must first be washed thoroughly in warm soapy water, then rinsed in clear water. Any debris or matter in the shell apertures should be removed with a brush. The shells will be enhanced if they are soaked (about a minute for small shells up to an hour for larger ones) in a solution of chlorine bleach combined with water. Rinse the bleach off the shells and wash them again.

To give them luster, rub the shells with baby oil or machine oil, cut with lighter fluid. Paste the shells to the background.

Shell flowers should be made first on a disc base which is later glued to the background. The size of the disc is determined by the size of the flower it will hold. If necessary, the shells should be drilled first to make a hole near their base. A fine wire can be strung though each hole, and the wires can then be fastened into holes made in the disc. Use a fast-drying glue; stores selling shells have all the necessary materials.

EDGAR ALLAN POE MUSEUM
RICHMOND, VIRGINIA — 1685-1688

In this, the oldest dwelling in the City of Richmond, collectors have brought together rare Poe relics: his trunk which held his possessions at the time of his death; his cane and boot hooks, his wife's trinket box, and handsome furnishings from the home of his foster mother, Mrs. Frances Valentine Allan. (When Poe's mother, the British-born Elizabeth Arnold Poe, died in December, 1811, the boy became the adopted son of the Allans, from whom he took his middle name.)

The Old Stone House and adjacent buildings are now owned by the Association for the Preservation of Virginia Antiquities. Under their aegis, a scale model of the Richmond in which the haunted poet lived and worked is exhibited.

Below   Red azaleas and camellias, pink flowering plum, and eucalyptus are arranged in an old pewter container on an early pine stretcher table. A pine Jamestown cupboard in the background displays pewter ware.

Opposite   The Thomas Jefferson Garden Club of Richmond restored the Enchanted Garden at the Museum in 1956, winning an award for civic beautification presented by the Richmond Council of Garden Clubs.

WESTBURY HOUSE AND GARDENS
OLD WESTBURY, NEW YORK — GEORGIAN 1906

Westbury House was designed by the British architect, George Crawley, for the late financier and sportsman, John S. Phipps, and his wife Margarita Grace, and it was here in 1953, surrounded by their children and grandchildren, that the Phipps celebrated their golden wedding anniversary. The property was originally part of a large tract of land owned by the horticulturally renowned Hicks family. Mr. Phipps bought part of the land in 1901 and acquired more later. The gardens, rich with lakes, pools, formal flower beds and miles of winding paths, exemplify the gracious living of the early part of this century; they are maintained as a nonprofit arboretum and horticultural exhibit by the Board of Directors of the Old Westbury Gardens Foundation.

The interior of Westbury House, furnished now with pieces the same as or similar to those used when the family occupied it, is a setting for fine English furniture and *objets d'art* of the eighteenth and earlier centuries with paintings by Joshua Reynolds, Thomas Gainsborough, and John Singer Sargent.

Opposite   A glass enclosed west porch was added to the house by George Crawley in 1924. Its great oak beams, from which hang light fixtures made from solid alabaster, are supported on classic columns above a marble floor. Mahogany Chinese Chippendale-style armchairs are scattered throughout. French terra cotta cupids are similar to statuary found throughout the garden. A magnificent spreading beech tree frames the view outdoors. Mrs. Phipps' interest in flowers and gardens is apparent throughout this Westbury estate, but nowhere more than in this pleasant porch room which adjoined her study. Here, Chinese Ming bronze jardinieres are filled wih ferns, and masses of pink and white flowers echo the colors in the flowered slipcovers on the deeply padded upholstered sofas.

Following page   The house has many fine mantelpieces, but none is considered a more splendid work of art than the one in the elegant oak-paneled dining room. It is faced with verde antico bolection molding, and two white marble caryatids uphold the white marble mantelpiece. Grinling Gibbons executed the vertical wood carvings on either side of the Gainsborough painting of the Duke of Clarence above the fireplace; among the clusters of fruits and vegetables are the pea pods which Grinling often used as his signature. The Louis XV mantel clock is painted and ornamented wood and gilded copper.

Around the dining table are walnut Georgian arm and side chairs. The centerpiece is a mass of carnations mounded to suggest a fluffy cake. A silver-plated repoussé chandelier with eighteen lights is suspended over the table; the wall lights, copied from William and Mary sconces, were made by Francis Derwent Wood, a friend of George Crawley.

NATHANIAL RUSSELL HOUSE
CHARLESTON, SOUTH CAROLINA — FEDERAL c. 1807

The Nathaniel Russell House is one of the finest town houses of the Federal period, owing much of its charm and beauty to the Adam style which was in fashion at the time it was built. This house, important for beautiful interior detail, was restored by hte Historic Charleston Foundation in 1956.

Below   In the rounded end of the library, an arrangement in warm gold to brown tones designed by Mrs. Ellison A. Williams is set in a bronze bowl on a Sheraton-style drum table. Beech leaves and dock frame and emphasize the dried hydrangea and celosia in the focal area.

OLD STURBRIDGE VILLAGE
STURBRIDGE, MASSACHUSETTS — 1790-1840

Old Sturbridge Village is not a restoration, but the re-creation of an imaginary New England community representative of the period 1790-1840. Its purposes are historical and educational: "to preserve and present the story of New England farm and village life of yesterday and to impart a knowledge and understanding of that heritage to the citizens of today," according to a recent annual report of the Trustees of Old Sturbridge Village.

The story of the Village began in the 1920's when the brothers Albert B. Wells and J. Cheney Wells caught the collecting fever. As the fame of their collection spread, it became apparent that their private treasures — chairs, clocks, axes, hinges, copper, and brass — were of considerable public interest. The 20 acres of the present village site on the Quinebaug River were acquired to form the ponds for the saw and grist mills, and thirty buildings of a typical village were moved in to become showcases for the smaller items.

The Village, now managed by a professional museum staff, is an independent nonprofit educational institution established as a bequest from the brothers. First opened to the public in 1946, twenty years later it is visited annually by nearly half a million people.

The farmhouse built by Pliny Freeman in 1801 had only two rooms in the *Opposite* main part of the house — upstairs and downstairs. The rear extension, shown here, has its own chimney with kitchen, buttery, and storage shed. Although the fields were usually planted with grains and vegetables, the kitchen gardens were tended by the women who, in addition to raising peas, lettuce, berries, squash, beans, and greens, often grew such favorite flowers as iris, lemon lilies, phlox, roses, and others. The homestead was normally stocked with a pair of oxen, four to eight cows, twelve or fourteen sheep, a few swine, and assorted chickens, geese, dogs, and cats; few farmers had horses.

In 1796, General Salem Towne built this fine house in Carlton, Massachu- *Below* setts, a square Federal mansion with an entrance on each of its four sides. This view from the garden with its formal beds of herbs shows the house's most unusual feature, its monitor roof, which allows light to enter the attic through a series of small windows. The two chimneys on either side of a central hall provide a fireplace for each of the four rooms upstairs and down.

OATLANDS
LEESBURG, VIRGINIA — FEDERAL 1800-1803.

When George Carter came of age, he received 5,000 acres from his father, who in 1776 had purchased 63,093 acres from the estate of Lord Fairfax, proprietor of land at the northern neck of Virginia. In building Oatland Mills, as it was called in 1800, George drew heavily on *A Treatise on Civil Architecture in Which the Principles of That Art Are Laid Down* by William Chambers, published in London in 1768, to create a Federal mansion with formal gardens. Oatlands' bricks were molded and fired on the property, and the timbers were cut from its forests.

The fortunes of the family declined until the house was sold. In 1903, Mr. and Mrs. William C. Eustis purchased the property and, using the Chambers *Treatise* as well as the original garden plans, started restoration. The huge stone steps in the garden were repaired. The ruined slave quarters were removed, and the garden, made into parterres, was extended to the terrace which the Eustises enclosed on the south and east with a balustrade.

When Mrs. Eustis died in 1964, her daughters donated the house, furnishings, gardens, and 261 acres of adjacent property to the National Trust with

an endowment for the preservation and maintenance of the house and gardens as a memorial to their parents.

The entrance door has a definite Adamesque character in the leaded tracery at the side windows, the overdoor lunette, and in the entablature frieze below the cornice.   *Opposite*

Through the opening in the ancient Carter boxwood along one of the gravel paths, tulips bloom in the formal garden at Oatlands. Mrs. Eustis had the bowling green transformed into a boxwood *allée* with a pool at one end and a summer house at the other, and she had parterres and terraces designed to surround architectural artifacts brought from Europe.   *Below*

STAN HYWET FOUNDATION
AKRON, OHIO — ENGLISH TUDOR REVIVAL

Below   This magnificent house (1911-1915) was inspired by Ochwells Manor, forty miles from London. During the planning stage, groups of architects, decorators and landscape designers were transported to England a number of times to see the Manor and to select furnishings for the American counterpart. The house is of handmade English bricks with white sandstone moldings and slate roofs; the entrance resembles the one at the castle of Henry the Eighth. Over the door, a stone coat of arms proclaims *Non Nobis Solum* (*Not for Us Alone*). Sixty-five rooms include a forty-foot swimming pool, a big game room, and a spacious gymnasium in a remote part of the building where the six children of the household could play without disturbing the adult members of the family.

The builder of this remarkable mansion was F. A. Seiberling, who developed various rubber articles for the Goodyear Tire and Rubber Company, which he founded. In 1921, at the age of sixty-one, having lost a twenty million dollar fortune and the board chairmanship of his company, he went on to found the Seiberling Rubber Company and establish another fortune.

After the deaths of Mr. and Mrs. Seiberling (he died in 1955, aged ninety-

five), the house was given to the city of Akron, which administers it today as a tax-free public shrine. An admission fee is for maintenance of the mansion and the thirty-eight acres of gardens which are open daily.

The name Stan Hywet means stone quarry, but the original quarries on the property are now filled with water to provide pools for fishing, skating, swimming, boating, and reflecting the beauty of the ever-changing seasons. A professional Shakespeare company usually performs on the terraces in July and August, with Juliet leaning from one of the balconies. Minstrel groups and string ensembles are followed by modern concerts and jazz bands, with an occasional antique car show.

To fulfill the requirement for an oriental design, Mrs. Kazuko Yonetsu made *Below left* a traditional Japanese arrangement using flowering plum branches which echo those in the hanging scroll. The prescribed heaven-man-earth lines and the authentic *usabata* container complete the assignment.

Mrs. S. D. Stanson made an arrangement in the classic style of early Greece. *Below right* She used an Etruscan cup on a pedestal with a marble base; the vines, wheat, carnations, lilies, and other flowers bring brilliant color to the rich quiet paneling of the library.

Below   Mrs. Frank McCormish created a graceful pastel mass arrangement in eighteenth-century style. The Dresden pitcher holds gladioli, irises, peonies, carnations, snapdragons, and wild flowers.

Above opposite   Mrs. Ray Adey has combined bleeding heart, daisies, lemon lilies, flax, and other garden flowers in the traditional Flemish flower art: even a bird's nest is here. (Flemish artists painted great masses of flowers with stuffed birds, moths, butterflies, and speckled birds' eggs to show natural cycles.) The Spanish altar candles of gold and enamel are ornamented with tiny mirrors and bits of glass. This setting is in an alcove in the beautiful music room which seats four hundred spectators. Here many famed artists have performed, including Rosa Ponselle, Ernestine Schumann-Heink, Amelita Galli-Curci, Ignace Jan Paderewski, and others.

Below opposite   In the intimate breakfast room, Mrs. T. J. Dietry assembled charming early summer flowers in the Victorian manner. She included iris, bleeding heart, dictamus, oriental poppies, columbine, clematis, lupine, cornflowers, wood phlox, variegated weigela, and others. A page from a Victorian manuscript makes an interesting accessory.

Below   Mrs. A. B. Arrington planned a composition in a romantic mood. The massed-line arrangement, predominantly French in feeling, draws the eye from the painting to the Jacobean desk, the intricately carved chair, and the ornamented desk accessories. Yellow roses, daisies, pansies, and spiral eucalyptus are the plant materials.

TYRON PALACE

NEW BERN, NORTH CAROLINA — COLONIAL 1767-1770

Below   Tyron Palace was the first permanent capitol of North Carolina. Its many gardens are designed in the manner of eighteenth-century English gardens to blend with the restored British Colonial capitol building. This view of the Maude Moore Latham Memorial Garden shows tulips and other eighteenth-century flowers and shrubs bordered by dwarf yaupon. At the right is a memorial pavilion with a plaque to Mrs. Latham, who donated the money to restore the capitol. In the rear is the west wing of the Palace, the main building, and the reconstructed eighteenth-century dovecote.

98

DECATUR HOUSE
WASHINGTON, D. C. — LATE GEORGIAN 1819

Thirty-seven-year-old Stephen Decatur came to Washington, D. C., in 1816 rich with prize money from having subdued the pirate ships of Algiers, Tunis, and Tripoli. He bought nineteen lots on the President's Square and, choosing the one opposite the northwest corner of the square for its setting, he commissioned Benjamin Henry Latrobe, America's first professional architect, to design his townhouse.

Commodore Decatur and his wife, Susan Wheeler, lived in the house 14 months, making it the social center of Washington. On March 22, 1820, Decatur fought a fatal duel with Commodore James Barron. Susan deserted the house at once, but did not sell it for many years.

After the death of Decatur the house was occupied by the French Legation, the Russian Legation, and later by the British ministry. Three Secretaries of State lived in Decatur House—Henry Clay, Edward Livingston, and Martin Van Buren, who later became President.

In 1877, Decatur House was purchased by Mary Edwards Beale, wife of General Edward Fitzgerald Beale. In 1956, Mrs. Truxton Beale, widow of the General's son, having restored Decatur House according to the eleven original Latrobe drawings, bequeathed it to the National Trust.

Opposite

Masses of *Magnolia grandiflora* leaves set off with chrysanthemums in Nanking China flower stands flank the door in the main entrance of Decatur House.

Following page

The portrait over the fireplace in a sitting room is the General's father, George Beale, who was presented a silver medal by Congress for "gallantry, good conduct and services" in the decisive and splendid victory on Lake Champlain, September, 1814, over a British squadron of superior force. In summer, sumac, grasses, and dried yellow flowers chosen to harmonize with the color of the painted wall conceal the fireplace opening, which is flanked by Chippendale and Hepplewhite chairs appropriate to the gracious Georgian setting.

OLANA
HUDSON, NEW YORK — 1870-1872

Olana (the name is Arabic for "Our Place on High") is a Moorish-Italian villa built for Frederic Edwin Church, the famous nineteenth-century landscape artist. The house and its furnishings ranging from a Duncan Phyfe sofa to oriental pottery to an exotic Persian taboret show Church's individualistic tastes and cultural interests.

Below In this gallery which connects the library with Church's studio hangs a verdure tapestry of a garden scene. Woodwork carvings consist of leaf and tendril motifs. The portrait by Charles Loring Elliot is of the artist's father.

WILCOX HOUSE
YORK, MAINE — MID-EIGHTEENTH CENTURY

Wilcox House was used as a residence, tailor shop, general store, taproom, stagecoach stop, and post office. Several old York families have lived here at times; their descendants still live in York. The Old Gaol Museum Committee has furnished the house with rooms of the period 1740-1840: Queen Anne, Chippendale, Sheraton, Hepplewhite, and Duncan Phyfe. One curious room is furnished with furniture and objects from China that a former owner of the house brought back on his Clipper ship in the 1840's.

Across the burying ground is the Gaol itself, from which the committee takes its name. Built by the British in 1653, it is the oldest public building in the United States still in use. Besides dungeons and cells, there are living quarters for the "gaoler" and his wife.

Below   The copper luster pitcher in the hall is filled with marigolds, cornflowers, and goldenrod arranged by a member of the Old York Garden Club. Simple bouquets reminiscent of the period in which the house was built are kept in the sitting room and the dining room by the garden-club members.

JACOB FORD MANSION

MORRISTOWN, NEW JERSEY — 1772

When the Revolutionary War began, Morristown was a small rural community with about fifty houses and a few churches and shops. Although only thirty miles from the enemy lines in New York and Staten Island, the town was well protected by the Watchung Mountains. During the winter of 1779-80, Washington systematically reorganized his weary depleted forces and, in the face of bitter cold, hunger, hardshrip and disease, sustained and developed the nation's will to gain independence and freedom.

During this terrible winter, Washington made his headquarters at the mansion built just before the conflict began by Colonel Jacob Ford, Jr., landowner, iron manufacturer, and patriot. Architecturally, the house is of the symmetrical Paladian design, particularly its beautiful main doorway.

Below   The building was partially restored by the National Park Service in 1939 and is now furnished with authentic pieces of the 1780 period. The American mahogany table has three cabriole legs which terminate in drake feet. The Chippendale wing chair and the draperies are of a rich green-gold wool damask made in England. Mrs. Thomas Cooke has arranged marigolds, celosia, and dusty miller in various tones of the same green-gold to complete the grouping in the upstairs main hall.

103

WATERLOO VILLAGE
STANHOPE, NEW JERSEY — 1760, 1838, 1859

When the Dutch came to America, part of the narrow valley along the Musconetcong River between the Allamuchy and Schooley's Mountain Ranges was owned by William Penn and his brother. About 1760 a section of this land was sold to two Englishmen, Allen and Turner, who three years later set up a blast furnace refinery and forge, the nucleus of Andover Forge. After the Battle of Waterloo in 1815, English sympathizers in the village changed the town's name to Waterloo, but by this time the forests had been denuded to feed the greedy furnace and forge; the iron industry had literally burned itself up.

In 1824 the Morris Canal and Bonding Company was formed to build a canal for transporting coal and iron more profitably. When the canal was completed at Waterloo, John Smith and his sons built the store, gristmill, plaster mill, and opened a tavern which became a social center and political arena. The store did a $75,000 business in a peak year. But the canal was too narrow and shallow to accommodate large boats, and in 1865 the canal was replaced by the Morris and Essex Railroad which ran from Newark to Phillips-burg. The once thriving town began to decline, and up until the shortage of housing following the Second World War, the village was relatively deserted. Bought recently by Mr. Percival H. E. Leach and Mr. Louis D. Gualandi, the village has been revived and houses have been restored and refurnished in styles typical of their varied periods.

Below   An old stone building, now called Canal House, was built for two families

between 1724 and 1730. When restored recently, a Hessian sword, an interesting remnant of Revolutionary days, was found in its walls.

Below

The Old Stage Coach Inn was built in 1740 to accommodate passengers going from Phillipsburg, Pennsylvania, to Albany, New York, and one night there was a record crowd of fifty-six patrons. Today's view of the dining room shows the tavern table; around it are Dorchester banister-back chairs probably two hundred and fifty years old. Dried wheat grasses, thistle heads, and celosia are massed in a small copper kettle to provide color all winter. The cupboard in the background holds ironstone china marked *"Dieu et mon droit"* under a lion and unicorn beside a shield. This stoneware is English, although much of the decorated ware was marked with a similar crest at some of the potteries in this country.

Following page

An old carriage house is now used as a gift shop and drying loft. Bunches of globe amaranth, coxcomb, grasses, and goldenrod tied to bamboo poles hang upside down to dry. Many herbs and wild plants are dried here—costmary or Bible leaf to keep linens sweet and Bibles fresh; orange and lemon mint; horehound to make candy for coughs; sorrel for soups and salads; rue and wormwood (Artemisia camphorata) to keep moths out of linen; boneset for

tea to makes bones heal faster, bring down fever, and cure colds. The leaves of plantain (now such a pest in lawns) were originally used for a poultice to draw out infection and for poison ivy, and the seeds were used to make a tea for a kidney physic. Tansy for abortions, and pungent, minty pennyroyal to keep fleas, flies, and mosquitoes away. Beebalm tea for sore throats; goldenrod flowers for yellow dye and the leaves for a tonic tea or to worm children; feverfew against fever as the name implies; and Joe-Pye-weed, named after an old Indian that recommended it, as a cure-all. The horsetail rush was dried for polishing pewter and brewed into tea for diabetes; the marshmallow root could be cooked into a thick syrup to make medicine slide down more easily. Fennel was flavoring, and was sometimes brewed (with or without the addition of catnip) as a tea for a colicky baby. Yarrow tea for strength and endurance and its foliage to stop the bleeding of a wound. Rose hips, full of vitamin C, for tea or jelly. Chicory greens were used for salad and the roots were roasted along with barley and rye for coffee. Sunflower seeds were good for the stomach and eyes.

Opposite   In the dining room of Wellington House, the table is set with Waterford crystal and Crown Staffordshire gold dining plates on silver service plates. Babies'-breath and roses fill the top of an epergne (and bowls on each side); fruits in season are mounded in the lower tier of the epergne. The crystal chandelier has been wired for electricity.

LYNDHURST
TARRYTOWN, NEW YORK — GOTHIC REVIVAL 1838

This house is a nineteenth-century architectural document with its pictur-esque towers, turrets, gables, and pinnacles. "Hudson River Gothic", it was designed by Alexander Jackson Davis in 1838 for William Paulding and en-larged in 1865 by George Merritt, its second owner. The house was purchased by Jay Gould in 1880 and left to the National Trust in 1964 by one of his daughters, Anne, Duchess of Talleyrand-Perigord, to be operated as a nonprofit museum.

Below First Paulding's library, next Merritt's billiard room, and finally Gould's art gallery, this handsome room now houses Gould's greatly expanded display of art treasures. The open-timbered roof with haunched beams is supported on cast-stone corbels depicting the faces of Shakespeare, Washington, and other historic characters. Over the enormous stained-glass window at one end of the room is a lunette admitting daylight to highlight the roof carvings. Oriental rugs conceal parts of the parquet floor. Radiators are hidden behind elaborate cast-iron façades with marble tops. On the library table by Davis is a casual spray arrangement of pink flowering cherry blossoms. Other bunches of flowers repeat the colors of the paintings of the nineteenth-century French school, in-cluding one by Corot. Great ring chandeliers (about 1865) provide lighting at night.

Opposite In the dining room, the great room of Mr. Merritt's additions, the woodwork and walls—through new graining, marbleizing, stenciling, and painting—have been restored as nearly as possible to original appearances. Clustered engaged columns painted to match the marble of the fireplace support the ceiling. Wooden tracery around the top of the walls duplicates that of the stained glass windows. The leather-covered Gothic chairs, designed by Mr. A. Davis for the original house, cluster around the table sumptuously set with candles, flowers, and tiers of fruit.

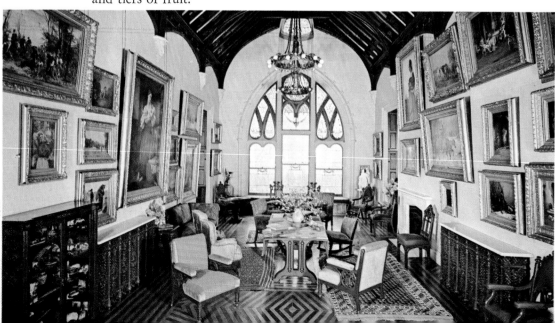

JOHN BROWN HOUSE
PROVIDENCE, RHODE ISLAND — 1786

The John Brown House is the present headquarters of The Rhode Island Historical Society, who have taken great care with every detail, even reproducing the exact shade of wall paint used in the original house.

Below   Flanking a rare shelf clock made by Seril Dodge in Providence (1785-1800) are arrangements by Mrs. O. Griswold Boynton for this second floor northwest room. Eucalyptus (preserved in glycerine), red roses, and one pink bridesmaid rose (dried in silica gel) are shown in bronze containers.

Opposite   Yellow roses, blue salvia, and rosemary for remembrance—all preserved by silica gel—bloom all winter in a Wedgwood digital vase on a mantel above one of the twelve fireplaces in the house. This one in a bedroom on the second floor is faced with white marble with mahogany enframement and has a lovely Adam mantel with a swag motif carved from pine. All the cornices, friezes, pediments, and mantels are elaborately carved, giving the mansion great elegance.

On this Massachusetts lowboy is a dried bouquet of yellow statice, green and white hydrangeas, yellow marigolds and purple clematis arranged by Mrs. O. Griswold Boynton. The looking glass in this bedroom descended through the Saltonstall-Greenleaf-Quincy families.

Opposite

This mantel in the morning room is flanked by arched windows. In beautiful scale with it and picking up the color of the export plates is this dried arrangement of blue delphinium, white lilacs and hydrangeas, roses, and mahonia foliage. Mahogany, here used to embellish the mantel, is lavishly used throughout the house.

Below

Dried roses, white statice, and glycerinized cedar are arranged in an alabaster urn by Mrs. O. Griswold Boynton as a perfect harmony for the pastel portrait of Anna Cooke, daughter of Nicholas Cooke, Rhode Island's Revolutionary War governor. The bowfront chest of drawers was made in Providence in 1810 by Joseph Rawson, Sr.

Following page

Glycerinizing is a method used for preserving foliage. Leaves of aspidistra, autumn oak, barberry, beech, canna, cedar, dogwood, eucalyptus, eleagnus, mahonia, and rhododendron are among those which respond to this treatment. Some leaves turn a lovely bright red, others remain relatively unchanged in color but take on a smooth glossy texture. Most leaves treated this way will last for years.

To glycerinize leaves, cut branches on a dry day, remove damaged leaves, and split or pound the stems to increase intake of the liquid. Stand the stems in a jar containing one part of glycerine to two parts of water. After two to five weeks, when the glycerine has been absorbed and the leaves feel supple, remove them and use in flower arrangements. Store in boxes when not needed. The glycerine can be reused; just add water.

METROPOLITAN MUSEUM OF ART

NEW YORK, NEW YORK

Benkard Room—Federal

Mrs. Harry Horton Benkard of Oyster Bay, Long Island, New York, was a discriminating collector of antiques and after her death her friends purchased her parlor and donated it to the Metropolitan Museum of Art.

Below   The elegance of the room derives from the silver blue and muted plum satin damask upholstery and drapes, the handsome Federal furniture, and the perfect scale of the furnishings to the background. Mrs. Benkard acquired the paneling for the room from the Smith-Nichols House when it was about to be demolished in 1937. The paneling is a successful combination of Colonial and neoclassical styles with a bold scale cornice and dado. The candlesticks on the Baltimore secretary-bookcase were purchased by Mrs. Benkard's grandparents in 1845. The drapery used throughout the room—above the windows, behind the glass of the secretary, and on the back of the sofa—are copied from Sheraton's drawing book. The chairs and the sofa with its motif of carved fans, as well as the drapery, are typical of Manhattan's early classical revival. The sewing table and Martha Washington chair (a duplicate of one owned by John Adams) have the spare, shapely outline and lightly incised carving of

the Massachusetts cabinetmakers. Note the accessories: the blue Chinese export porcelain which here holds masses of dried flowers, the Sheffield silver lamp bases made in 1790 to burn whale oil, and the rare ivory chess set on the Federal chess table. The elegant chandelier, so appropriate to the room, has a diamond pattern cut in the shaft and arms.

Below At the other end of the room, ornate gold and mahogany mirrors reflect the girandoles. The pair of card tables flanking the fireplace has geometric and bell-flower inlays of contrasting colored wood like the chess table in the preceding photograph. The painting over the mantel is of the tragic battle and surrender of the U. S. frigate *President,* commanded by Stephen Decatur, on January 15, 1815, three weeks after the signing of the Treaty of Ghent.

Opposite Quillwork was an art highly developed among some tribes of North American Indians who worked colored porcupine quills into elaborate designs on a background of skins, bark, or fabric. Similar decorations were taught at fashionable schools of the eighteenth century, and it is easy to imagine the young girls of a family working during the winter evenings, folding, rolling, and curling paper into the required fancy shapes. The paper was painted or gilded and carefully glued into place with hundreds of other three-dimensional small pieces—bits of mica, shells, dried flowers, spirals of wire, even tiny figures, all

in harmonious relationship. They were usually framed in shadow boxes (as in the Brush-Everard House of Colonial Williamsburg listed in index), but were sometimes used as the back plates of wall candle sconces. The brass candleholder (c. 1720) is one of a pair. It is decorated with a vase of flowers including mica, shells, and silver and copper wire, and framed in gilt wood.

117

INDEX